Flying Starters

Words and Writing

BARDFIELD
PRESS

First published in 2005 by Bardfield Press

Bardfield Press is an imprint of
Miles Kelly Publishing Ltd
Bardfield Centre, Great Bardfield,
Essex, CM7 4SL

British Library Cataloguing-in-Publication Data. A catalogue record for this book is available from the British Library

ISBN 1-84236-547-9

2 4 6 8 10 9 7 5 3 1

Editorial Director: Belinda Gallagher

Project Manager: Lisa Clayden

Editorial Assistant: Amanda Askew

Production Manager: Estela Boulton

Design: Mackerel Ltd

Questions: Brian Williams

Cartoons: Mark Davis

Contact us by email:
info@mileskelly.net

Visit us on the web:
www.mileskelly.net

Printed in China

How to use this book

Your book is split into 28 quizzes, each containing ten multiple-choice questions. There are six subject categories for you to choose from. Simply write your answers in pencil in the answer panel. Turn to page 32 to check your answers. Rub out your answers and try again! You can chart your progress by using the score sheet at the back of the book.

Icons
See below for a key to these icons

Questions

Answer options

Cartoon clue

Your Answer
Write your answer here

Book Answer
Tick or cross your answer

Quiz Score
Write your total out of 10

Key to subject icons

Books and stories

Writing

Sounds and rhymes

Word meanings

Spellings

Grammar

Quiz 1

Your answer | Book answer

1. What is used to haul up a heavy weight on a rope?
(a) **Windlass** (b) **Anchor** (c) **Cutlass** (d) **Windmill**

2. Something to sit on:
(a) **Sopha** (b) **Sofa** (c) **Sofer** (d) **Sewfeh**

3. How do you spell what a cook does with meat?
(a) **Rust** (b) **Roost** (c) **Roast** (d) **Rewst**

4. Which word rhymes with 'groove'?
(a) **Move** (b) **Love** (c) **Cave** (d) **Dive**

5. An adjective that means 'being very lazy':
(a) **Glutton** (b) **Anger** (c) **Slothful** (d) **Jealous**

6. Who is the boy who found the Golden Ticket in a chocolate bar?
(a) **William** (b) **Peter Pan** (c) **Oliver Twist** (d) **Charlie Bucket**

7. The proof of the pudding is in the…what (saying)?
(a) **Eating** (b) **Crust** (c) **Pizza** (d) **Baking**

8. 'What is 'pram' short for?
(a) **Pusher** (b) **Perambulator** (c) **Parameter** (d) **Pedalamabus**

9. What's another word for a flat (for living in)?
(a) **Level** (b) **Apartment** (c) **Cellar** (d) **Attic**

10. A group of witches:
(a) **Gaggle** (b) **Herd** (c) **Coven** (d) **Clutch**

Quiz 1 score

Quiz 2

Q4

Your answer | Book answer

1. A stamp collector:
(a) **Archaeologist** (b) **Philatelist** (c) **Twitcher** (d) **Trainspotter**

Q2

2. A word meaning 'feeling sick':
(a) **Hysteria** (b) **Vertigo** (c) **Claustrophobia** (d) **Nausea**

3. Find the noun here:
(a) **Meal** (b) **Mild** (c) **Mincing** (d) **Milled**

4. What should you beware of in a field?
(a) **Sheep** (b) **Bull** (c) **Tractor** (d) **Hayrick**

5. In which book does the Wild Wood feature?
(a) **Wind in the Willows** (b) **Badger's Mount** (c) **Mole's Return** (d) **Toad Hall**

6. A Roald Dahl character: the Big Friendly...?
(a) **Giant** (b) **Rat** (c) **Dog** (d) **Martian**

Q8

7. Which is the female horse?
(a) **Folly** (b) **Fetlock** (c) **Furlong** (d) **Filly**

8. Find the consonant:
(a) **E** (b) **O** (c) **S** (d) **U**

9. What is the plural of country?
(a) **Country** (b) **Countries** (c) **Countrys** (d) **Countryes**

10. Which word means 'put back as it was'?
(a) **Repulsed** (b) **Refreshed** (c) **Created** (d) **Restored**

Quiz 2 score

Quiz 3

Q10

Your answer | Book answer

1. Which of these was a Russian writer?
(a) **Tolstoy** (b) **Dickens** (c) **Twain** (d) **Burns**

Q3

2. Which is the adverb?
(a) **Bright** (b) **Brightness** (c) **Brightly** (d) **Brighter**

3. A person looking on is a ... what?
(a) **Pedestrian** (b) **Spectator** (c) **Terrestrial** (d) **Motorist**

4. A loud bang:
(a) **Examination** (b) **Exhibition** (c) **Explanation** (d) **Explosion**

5. The plural of lesson is ...what?
(a) **Lesson** (b) **Lessones** (c) **Lesson's** (d) **Lessons**

6. Sarah was very happy, she was ... what?
(a) **Exasperated** (b) **Exhausted** (c) **Excited** (d) **Ecstatic**

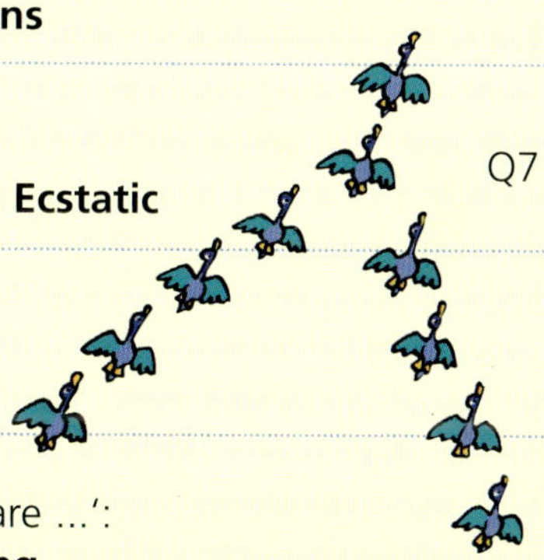

Q7

7. One goose, ten ... what?
(a) **Gooses** (b) **Geese** (c) **Gice** (d) **Geeses**

8. Complete this sentence to make sense: 'Coal fires are ...':
(a) **Good to eat** (b) **Electric** (c) **Hot** (d) **Freezing**

9. What do you get in a shop after paying?
(a) **Recipe** (b) **Receipt** (c) **Record** (d) **Remedy**

10. What does a plagiarist do?
(a) **Collect shells** (b) **Lie on the beach** (c) **Copy someone's work**
(d) **Tell lies**

Quiz 3 score

Quiz 4

Q2

Your answer | Book answer

1. As ... as a lion (proverb):
(a) **Fat** (b) **Brave** (c) **Deaf** (d) **Silent**

2. Who wrote plays for the Globe Theatre?
(a) **Byron** (b) **Austen** (c) **Shakespeare** (d) **Ayckbourne**

3. Which isn't a punctuation mark?
(a) **Division sign** (b) **Full stop** (c) **Colon** (d) **Question Mark**

4. Fill in the missing word in the book title: The Worst ... :
(a) **Teacher** (b) **Goalkeeper** (c) **Astronaut** (d) **Witch**

5. Everything and everywhere:
(a) **Underground** (b) **Universe** (c) **Untidy** (d) **University**

Q9

6. What scared Little Miss Muffet?
(a) **Dragon** (b) **Spider** (c) **Toadstool** (d) **Witch**

7. Which of these is a preposition?
(a) **By** (b) **Moving** (c) **Clever** (d) **Tom**

8. Easy ... what (saying)?
(a) **Peasy** (b) **Greasy** (c) **Measly** (d) **Weesy**

9. Spell a word that means 'not very clever':
(a) **Stoopid** (b) **Stewpid** (c) **Stupid** (d) **Stupyd**

Q6

10. Which word rhymes with 'shiny'?
(a) **Tinny** (b) **Tiny** (c) **Slimy** (d) **Grimy**

Quiz 4 score

Quiz 5

Q4

Your answer | Book answer

Q10

1. Which spelling is correct for the day of the week?
   (a) **Toosday** (b) **Towsday** (c) **Tuesday** (d) **Twosday**

2. A book full of names and addresses:
   (a) **Journal** (b) **Dictionary** (c) **Directory** (d) **Atlas**

3. Which is wrong here?
   (a) **Ten dogs** (b) **Four cats** (c) **Ten beetle's** (d) **Fifteen cars**

4. Which spelling is correct?
   (a) **Hippopotamus** (b) **Hypopotamus** (c) **Hipopodamus** (d) **Hipperpottamoos**

5. Who went to London with his cat?
   (a) **Buttons** (b) **Dick Whittington** (c) **Aladdin** (d) **Peter Pan**

Q6

6. Something to ride on:
   (a) **Scooter** (b) **Skipper** (c) **Shopper** (d) **Slipper**

7. Word meaning to bear flowers:
   (a) **Sprout** (b) **Grow** (c) **Bloom** (d) **Wilt**

8. Which of these is correct?
   (a) **Sam's shoes** (b) **Sams shoes** (c) **Sams' shoe's** (d) **Sammes' shoes'**

9. Which word is a noun here?
   (a) **Run** (b) **Tent** (c) **Slowly** (d) **Terrible**

10. Mythical animal, half human and half horse:
    (a) **Centaur** (b) **Sentaur** (c) **Centore** (d) **Scentaur**

Quiz 5 score

Quiz 6

Q7

Your answer | Book answer

Q2

1. A word that means 'cross':
   (a) **Distraught** (b) **Irate** (c) **Dejected** (d) **Baffled**

2. What we do on holiday:
   (a) **Rellax** (b) **Relax** (c) **Reelacks** (d) **Rilacs**

3. The opposite of closed:
   (a) **Tight** (b) **Open** (c) **Undressed** (d) **Shut**

4. Which of these would you find in the kitchen?
   (a) **Spittoon** (b) **Spatula** (c) **Spade** (d) **Spreadsheet**

5. Which mark shows something belongs to someone?
   (a) **Apostrophe** (b) **Full stop** (c) **Exclamation mark** (d) **Question Mark**

Q10

6. What's the correct short form for 'you are'?
   (a) **You're** (b) **Your** (c) **Y'oure** (d) **Yo'are**

7. Which adjective goes best with 'elephant'?
   (a) **Enormous** (b) **Tiny** (c) **Slimy** (d) **Green**

8. Which writer created Winnie the Pooh?
   (a) **A.A. Milne** (b) **Richmal Crompton** (c) **Raymond Briggs** (d) **Roald Dahl**

9. Which marks show that someone is speaking?
   (a) **!** (b) **"** (c) **?** (d) **^**

10. Which is the correct plural?
    (a) **Slimy snail's** (b) **Slimys snails** (c) **Slimy snails** (d) **Slimeys snailes**

Quiz 6 score

Quiz 7

Q7

Your answer | Book answer

1. What might look 'as big as a mountain'?
(a) **A skyscraper** (b) **A house** (c) **A car** (d) **A chair**

Q4

2. Which word can mean 'lots of'?
(a) **Noodles** (b) **Poodles** (c) **Cuddles** (d) **Oodles**

3. What's another word for 'sea'?
(a) **Desert** (b) **Ocean** (c) **Lake** (d) **River**

4. Which word best describes a snake?
(a) **Dithering** (b) **Crouching** (c) **Slithering** (d) **Lurching**

5. What is the best word for a really exciting film?
(a) **Brilliant** (b) **Shiny** (c) **Boring** (d) **Long**

6. Which adjective might you use for a scrummy cake?
(a) **Delightful** (b) **Delicious** (c) **Detestable** (d) **Disgusting**

7. A word for an elephant's nose and a piece of luggage:
(a) **Tank** (b) **Bag** (c) **Snorkel** (d) **Trunk**

8. A letter to ask someone to a party is an:
(a) **Introduction** (b) **Imposition** (c) **Invitation** (d) **Inquisition**

9. Which word best describes the sound a cow makes?
(a) **Moo** (b) **Poo** (c) **Boo** (d) **Loo**

Q9

10. A long story in prose is a:
(a) **Novel** (b) **Sonnet** (c) **Opera** (d) **Symphony**

Quiz 7 score

Quiz 8

Q1

Your answer | Book answer

1. Which word is not a 'saying' word?
(a) **Whisper** (b) **Reply** (c) **Scratch** (d) **Scream**

2. Which word means 'quickly'?
(a) **Clumsily** (b) **Tidily** (c) **Sadly** (d) **Hurriedly**

3. A person in a story is a:
(a) **Character** (b) **Star** (c) **Producer** (d) **Author**

Q4

4. 'Jane sang loudly'; what part of speech is 'loudly'?
(a) **Verb** (b) **Adverb** (c) **Adjective** (d) **Noun**

5. A huge, hairy spider: how many adjectives?
(a) **Two** (b) **One** (c) **Three** (d) **None**

6. Which would 'creak' if you trod on them?
(a) **Grass** (b) **Slugs** (c) **Stairs** (d) **Carpet**

7. Which word sounds like something breaking?
(a) **Swish** (b) **Smash** (c) **Slosh** (d) **Slurp**

Q9

8. Mad Minnie moaned mournfully: which word is the verb?
(a) **Mad** (b) **Minnie** (c) **Moaned** (d) **Mournfully**

9. Which words mean to jump from a plane?
(a) **Bale out** (b) **Bowl out** (c) **Buck up** (d) **Belt up**

10. In which book do some pigs called Napoleon and Snowball appear?
(a) **Charlotte's Web** (b) **Ballet Shoes** (c) **Animal Farm** (d) **The Hobbit**

Quiz 8 score

Quiz 9

Q1

Your answer | Book answer

1. What's not a way of saying goodbye?
(a) **Bye-bye** (b) **So long** (c) **See you** (d) **Hi there**

2. A place for storing hay:
(a) **Barn** (b) **Burn** (c) **Bairn** (d) **Byre**

3. A word that means 'not very big':
(a) **Slanted** (b) **Stunted** (c) **Static** (d) **Sluggish**

Q6

4. An old-fashioned pen:
(a) **Scroll** (b) **Quill** (c) **Quilt** (d) **Parchment**

5. Which prefix means big?
(a) **Mini-** (b) **Mega-** (c) **Milli-** (d) **Micro-**

6. A noisy piece of sports equipment:
(a) **Rocket** (b) **Rabbit** (c) **Racket** (d) **Cracker**

7. What often shows a new paragraph?
(a) **A space** (b) **A full stop** (c) **A new page** (d) **A question mark**

Q4

8. Which word means a group of wolves?
(a) **Herd** (b) **Tribe** (c) **Pack** (d) **Flock**

9. In the past tense, I eat becomes ... what?
(a) **I eated** (b) **I ated** (c) **I eat'** (d) **I ate**

10. What's the comparative of 'old'?
(a) **Older** (b) **Ageing** (c) **Elderly** (d) **Oldest**

Quiz 9 score

Quiz 10

Q3

Your answer | Book answer

1. Find the noun or 'naming word':
(a) **Hedge** (b) **High** (c) **Horrible** (d) **Hungry**

Q4

2. Which word must always have a capital letter?
(a) **Year** (b) **Day** (c) **Sunday** (d) **Month**

3. Which of these is a noun?
(a) **Sleepy** (b) **Sleep** (c) **Slept** (d) **Sleeping**

4. Which of these means a group of sheep?
(a) **Flock** (b) **Flick** (c) **Fleck** (d) **Flurry**

5. Spell the plural of toy:
(a) **Toy's** (b) **Toy** (c) **Toys** (d) **Toyes**

6. How do you spell the 1st month of the year?
(a) **Jangywerry** (b) **Janyuarry** (c) **Jannurry** (d) **January**

Q8

7. Which of these is the infinitive of the verb?
(a) **Doing** (b) **To do** (c) **Done** (d) **Did**

8. To lose hair or feathers:
(a) **Melt** (b) **Mint** (c) **Mope** (d) **Moult**

9. Find the pronoun:
(a) **Him** (b) **Hungry** (c) **Henry** (d) **House**

10. Which is the object of the sentence in 'I neatly caught the red ball'?
(a) **I** (b) **Kicked** (c) **Neatly** (d) **The red ball**

Quiz 10 score

Quiz 11

Q2

Your answer | Book answer

1 Which word here always needs a capital N?
(a) **Number** (b) **Nicholas** (c) **Night** (d) **Next**

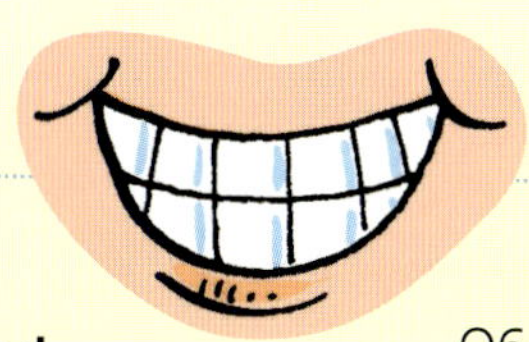

Q6

2 C.S. Lewis created this magical land:
(a) **Scotia** (b) **Toyland** (c) **Narnia** (d) **Never Never Land**

3 A bird and to complain:
(a) **Whinge** (b) **Grumble** (c) **Moan** (d) **Grouse**

4 Where does a full stop go?
(a) **End of a sentence** (b) **Start of a sentence** (c) **Middle of a sentence**
(d) **End of a piece of work**

5 Which of these shows a person is speaking?
(a) **Quote marks** (b) **Capital Letters** (c) **Question Mark** (d) **Apostrophe**

6 What's the plural of tooth?
(a) **Tooths** (b) **Toothes** (c) **Tooth** (d) **Teeth**

7 Who is the popular writer?
(a) **Freda Wilson** (b) **Wilma Wilson** (c) **Jacqueline Wilson** (d) **Wendy Wilson**

8 Place where butter is made:
(a) **Dairy** (b) **Diary** (c) **Laundry** (d) **Dictionary**

Q9

9 A kind of fish-eating bird:
(a) **Oyster** (b) **Osprey** (c) **Ostrich** (d) **Ocelot**

10 Which is the verb here?
(a) **Slid** (b) **Slippery** (c) **Slipper** (d) **Slingshot**

Quiz 11 score

Quiz 12

Q4

Your answer | Book answer

1. Which word means a long chunk of time?
(a) **Episode** (b) **Epoch** (c) **Epistle** (d) **Epitaph**

Q5

2. "HeyX" I shouted: what goes where the X is?
(a) **!** (b) **?** (c) **"** (d) **;**

3. Which of these is a storybook cat?
(a) **Spot** (b) **Bill** (c) **Rupert** (d) **Mog**

4. What's another word for 'fat'?
(a) **Stout** (b) **Stiff** (c) **Straight** (d) **Stuck-up**

5. Kylie has a kitten; the kitten is ... who's?
(a) **Kylies** (b) **Kylies'** (c) **Kyliees** (d) **Kylie's**

6. In which book do you start at Genesis?
(a) **Lord of the Rings** (b) **The Bible** (c) **Yellow Pages** (d) **Treasure Island**

7. What part of speech is 'quickly' in 'He dressed quickly'?
(a) **A noun** (b) **Adverb** (c) **Verb** (d) **Preposition**

8. Which missing letter or letters are shown by the apostrophe in 'It's raining'?
(a) **Was** (b) **i** (c) **o** (d) **might be**

Q10

9. How do you spell the capital of Scotland?
(a) **Eddyinbur** (b) **Edinburk** (c) **Edinburgh** (d) **Eddinburg**

10. What does claustrophobic mean?
(a) **Fear of heights** (b) **Fear of being shut in** (c) **Fear of clouds**
(d) **Fear of Santa Claus**

Quiz 12 score

Quiz 13

Q1

Your answer | Book answer

Q7

1. The opposite of fearful:
(a) **Scared** (b) **Fearless** (c) **Frail** (d) **Frightened**

2. Which word rhymes with 'cotton'?
(a) **Written** (b) **Kitten** (c) **Rotten** (d) **Curtain**

3. Which is wrong here?
(a) **Six sheep** (b) **Six cows** (c) **Six sheeps** (d) **Six dogs**

4. Another word for 'calm':
(a) **Cold** (b) **Silent** (c) **Placid** (d) **Painful**

5. Spell a nasty pain:
(a) **Ake** (b) **Ache** (c) **Hake** (d) **Ach**

Q6

6. An old word for a mad person:
(a) **Lunatic** (b) **Quack** (c) **Beggar** (d) **Footpad**

7. The skin of an apple:
(a) **Pile** (b) **Pith** (c) **Pelt** (d) **Peel**

8. Which word can mean 'easy'?
(a) **Sample** (b) **Simple** (c) **Sum** (d) **Single**

9. Shorten 'I will come' correctly:
(a) **I' w' come** (b) **Ill' come** (c) **I'll' come** (d) **I'll come**

10. The comparative of 'high' (adjective):
(a) **High** (b) **Highest** (c) **Higher** (d) **Highly**

Quiz 13 score

Quiz 14

Q7

	Your answer	Book answer
1 Find the adverb here: (a) **Slug** (b) **Slow** (c) **Slowness** (d) **Slowly**		
2 How many consonants in 'through'? (a) **Five** (b) **Two** (c) **Seven** (d) **None**		
3 Which of these would not be a compliment? (a) **Graceful** (b) **Handsome** (c) **Elegant** (d) **Hideous**		
4 What is a good word to describe peace and calm? (a) **Serene** (b) **Rowdy** (c) **Sad** (d) **Elegant**		
5 A place of worship: (a) **Mosk** (b) **Mosque** (c) **Mossk** (d) **Music**		
6 Which word could be a noun and a verb? (a) **Choose** (b) **Meat** (c) **Selection** (d) **Taste**		
7 'The hat of Molly'– which is correct here? (a) **Mollys hat** (b) **'Mollys hat** (c) **Mollys' hat** (d) **Molly's hat**		
8 Spell a word that means a sport: (a) **Affleticks** (b) **Afletics** (c) **Atheletics** (d) **Athletics**		
9 Which is wrong here? (a) **Six ships** (b) **Seven Seas** (c) **Four Buse's** (d) **Two toys**		
10 A word that describes a horse: (a) **Equal** (b) **Equine** (c) **Equinox** (d) **Equivalent**		

Q8

Quiz 14 score

Quiz 15

Q1

Your answer | Book answer

1. Which word rhymes with 'pleasant'?
(a) **Present** (b) **Pleasing** (c) **Pleasure** (d) **Feather**

2. What did Jack and Jill go up?
(a) **An escalator** (b) **A hill** (c) **A mountain** (d) **A windy road**

3. Which is not a verb here?
(a) **Swim** (b) **Float** (c) **Dive** (d) **Pond**

Q2

4. Opposite of 'honest':
(a) **Dishonest** (b) **Unhonest** (c) **Mishonest** (d) **Evil**

5. A verb and a carpenter's tool:
(a) **See** (b) **Saw** (c) **Sew** (d) **Sow**

6. Which spelling is correct here?
(a) **Ellyfant** (b) **Ellephant** (c) **Elephant** (d) **Helephant**

7. A well-known writer:
(a) **J.K. Rowling** (b) **J. Bowling** (c) **L.P. Mowling** (d) **I.M. Strolling**

8. Which pantomime starts with a cow being sold?
(a) **Dick Whittington** (b) **Aladdin** (c) **Jack and the Beanstalk**
(d) **Babes in the Wood**

9. Describes an animal that can swim or walk:
(a) **Amphitheatre** (b) **Ambidextrous** (c) **Amphibian** (d) **Ambulance**

10. Spell the name of a plant scientist:
(a) **Bottomist** (b) **Botonist** (c) **Bottenyst** (d) **Botanist**

Quiz 15 score

Quiz 16

Q5

Your answer | Book answer

1. Which of these is the infinitive of the verb?
(a) **Baking** (b) **To bake** (c) **Baked** (d) **I was baking**

2. What might you find on a table?
(a) **Cutlass** (b) **Cuttlefish** (c) **Cutlery** (d) **Cudgel**

3. Which is the adjective here?
(a) **Child** (b) **Children** (c) **Childish** (d) **Childishly**

4. Something used to show films:
(a) **Protester** (b) **Preparer** (c) **Producer** (d) **Projector**

5. People standing close together are in a ... what?
(a) **Huddle** (b) **Muddle** (c) **Cuddle** (d) **Puddle**

Q9

6. Which word means 'as clean as can be'?
(a) **Cleaner** (b) **Cleanier** (c) **Cleanish** (d) **Cleanest**

7. Which has the apostrophe in the right place?
(a) **Joes sock's** (b) **Jo'es socks** (c) **Joes socks'** (d) **Joe's socks**

8. What's the opposite of rough?
(a) **Smooth** (b) **Shiny** (c) **Clean** (d) **Smart**

9. What do we call a group of bees?
(a) **Flock** (b) **Swarm** (c) **Herd** (d) **School**

10. The past tense of 'I sing':
(a) **I sung** (b) **I song** (c) **I singed** (d) **I sang**

Q7

Quiz 16 score

Quiz 17

Q3

Your answer | Book answer

1. Which word rhymes with leather?
(a) **Weather** (b) **Either** (c) **Bother** (d) **Father**

2. Something that blocks up your nose:
(a) **Catmaran** (b) **Catalyst** (c) **Catarrh** (d) **Caterpillar**

3. Enid Blyton's famous … who?
(a) **Two** (b) **Four** (c) **Five** (d) **Fifteen**

4. 'As keen as …' what (saying)?
(a) **Mustard** (b) **Custard** (c) **Jam** (d) **Butter**

Q10

5. To try or write something in prose … (same word):
(a) **Foray** (b) **Essay** (c) **Melee** (d) **Souffle**

6. Opposite of proud:
(a) **Humble** (b) **Noble** (c) **Ignorant** (d) **Brave**

7. A kind of spear:
(a) **Harrow** (b) **Harp** (c) **Harpoon** (d) **Harpsichord**

8. Title of a famous book by George Orwell:
(a) **1900** (b) **1984** (c) **1894** (d) **2000**

9. To make a fuss:
(a) **Haggle** (b) **Goggle** (c) **Struggle** (d) **Niggle**

Q7

10. Which word means 'wandering '?
(a) **Erect** (b) **Erratic** (c) **Eroded** (d) **Evergreen**

Quiz 17 score

Quiz 18

Q4

Your answer | Book answer

1. A loud noise:
(a) **Din** (b) **Lilt** (c) **Tang** (d) **Aroma**

2. A writer's pen-name:
(a) **Disguise** (b) **Nom-de-plume** (c) **False beard** (d) **Alibi**

3. Part two of a film or book:
(a) **Epilogue** (b) **Introduction** (c) **Sequel** (d) **Chapter**

Q7

4. You hit this in a game of badminton:
(a) **Puck** (b) **Leather** (c) **Ball** (d) **Shuttlecock**

5. Tool with a curved blade for harvesting grain:
(a) **Sickle** (b) **Sickie** (c) **Cycle** (d) **Cygnet**

6. Spell 'a cunning plan':
(a) **Strattogerm** (b) **Stratagem** (c) **Strattygem** (d) **Stratterjen**

7. Spell a young cow:
(a) **Hepher** (b) **Heifer** (c) **Wether** (d) **Heffer**

Q5

8. Slang word meaning to run away:
(a) **Cop** (b) **Scarper** (c) **Scoff** (d) **Kip**

9. Not likely to study at Hogwarts?
(a) **Meanies** (b) **Muggles** (c) **Muppets** (d) **Misfits**

10. Adjective meaning 'from close range':
(a) **Hard and fast** (b) **Open–ended** (c) **Point blank** (d) **Hit and Miss**

Quiz 18 score

Quiz 19

Q2

Question	Your answer	Book answer
1 A forgetful, disorganized person: (a) **Brainbox** (b) **Scatterbrain** (c) **Chatterbox** (d) **Fidget**		
2 To go on board a ship: (a) **Embalm** (b) **Embed** (c) **Embezzle** (d) **Embark**		
3 What goes before 'face' to mean 'rub out'? (a) **ef-** (b) **in-** (c) **ex-** (d) **ab-**		
4 Which spelling is correct for a French hat? (a) **Berry** (b) **Beret** (c) **Beri** (d) **Beray**		
5 What would you do with a beverage? (a) **Drink it** (b) **Ride it** (c) **Wear it** (d) **Read it**		
6 Spell the plural of 'vase': (a) **Vasses** (b) **Vase's** (c) **Vasses'** (d) **Vases**		
7 An adjective meaning 'very strange': (a) **Shocking** (b) **Weird** (c) **Various** (d) **Frequent**		
8 Which of these is not a prefix? (a) **aero-** (b) **–archy** (c) **kilo-** (d) **ante-**		
9 Another word for a ghost: (a) **Wraith** (b) **Wreath** (c) **Wretch** (d) **Wrath**		
10 A collection of poems or stories: (a) **Encyclopedia** (b) **Epigram** (c) **Anthology** (d) **Index**		

Q5

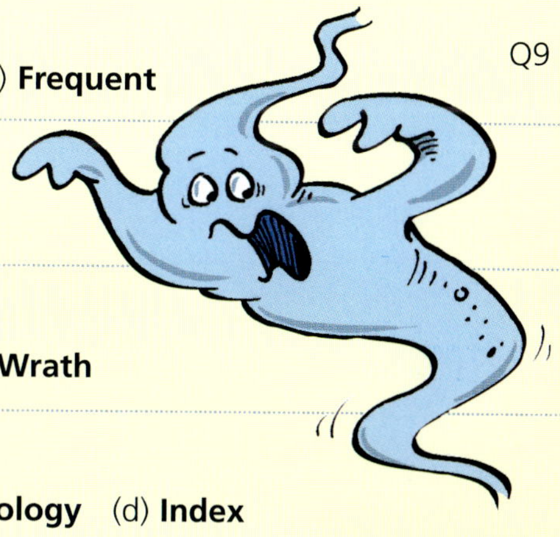

Q9

Quiz 19 score

Quiz 20

Q9

Your answer | Book answer

1. On a ship, for steering:
(a) **Ruff** (b) **Ruffle** (c) **Rudder** (d) **Rucksack**

2. Which word rhymes with weasel?
(a) **Woosle** (b) **Easel** (c) **Level** (d) **Weather**

3. To make fun of something or someone:
(a) **Copy** (b) **Admire** (c) **Compete** (d) **Mock**

Q2

4. Which of these is usually at the end of a book?
(a) **Prologue** (b) **Introduction** (c) **Title** (d) **Index**

5. To do with the eye:
(a) **Dental** (b) **Chronic** (c) **Optic** (d) **Mastic**

6. An ancient Greek shrine:
(a) **Oracle** (b) **Coracle** (c) **Monocle** (d) **Pyramid**

7. Spell someone who hopes for the best:
(a) **Pessimist** (b) **Optimist** (c) **Fortune-teller** (d) **Pesteemist**

8. To trick or fool someone:
(a) **To fox** (b) **To cow** (c) **To dog** (d) **To squirrel**

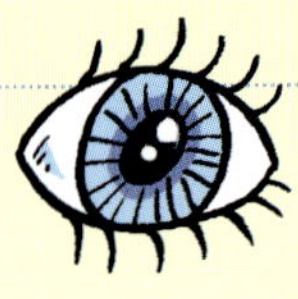

9. Spell the article of clothing:
(a) **Cloak** (b) **Cloke** (c) **Kloak** (d) **Clook**

Q5

10. Gloomy Dane in a play by Shakespeare:
(a) **Romeo** (b) **Othello** (c) **Lear** (d) **Hamlet**

Quiz 20 score

Quiz 21

Q1

Your answer | Book answer

1. A group of musicians:
(a) **Assembly** (b) **Ensemble** (c) **Platoon** (d) **Squadron**

2. A lot of fish:
(a) **Shoal** (b) **Formation** (c) **Gaggle** (d) **Herd**

Q2

3. Describes, or qualifies a noun:
(a) **Pronoun** (b) **Adverb** (c) **Adjective** (d) **Vowel**

4. Spell the musical instrument:
(a) **Xylophone** (b) **Zylophone** (c) **Seilophone** (d) **Silofone**

5. A word meaning 'to drive out':
(a) **Explain** (b) **Explode** (c) **Expel** (d) **Expect**

6. A word lots of us get wrong:
(a) **Nessessary** (b) **Necessury** (c) **Neccessery** (d) **Necessary**

7. Who wrote *A Christmas Carol*?
(a) **Dahl** (b) **Dickens** (c) **Shakespeare** (d) **Wordsworth**

Q7

8. Make an adjective from 'empire':
(a) **Imperial** (b) **Impressive** (c) **Impish** (d) **Impudent**

9. A child whose parents are dead:
(a) **Infant** (b) **Orphan** (c) **Evacuee** (d) **Stepchild**

10. Which does not mean the same as 'smart'?
(a) **Well-dressed** (b) **Clever** (c) **To be sore** (d) **To cheat**

Quiz 21 score

Quiz 22

Q1

Your answer | Book answer

1. Found in a playground:
(a) **Ho-hum** (b) **See-saw** (c) **Ha-ha** (d) **Bye-bye**

2. The past tense of 'to find':
(a) **Found** (b) **Funded** (c) **Finded** (d) **Fond**

Q3

3. Old-fashioned word for a chicken, or any bird:
(a) **Fowl** (b) **Kine** (c) **Steed** (d) **Brute**

4. What's the plural of 'fox'?
(a) **Foxen** (b) **Foxes** (c) **Foxs** (d) **Fox's**

5. Someone who looks after prisoners:
(a) **Wardrobe** (b) **Warrior** (c) **Warden** (d) **Warlock**

6. Rhymes with knife:
(a) **Strife** (b) **Knit** (c) **Living** (d) **Cliff**

7. Where a river starts:
(a) **Sorce** (b) **Sauce** (c) **Sortz** (d) **Source**

8. Means 'ball-shaped', but can you spell it?
(a) **Ferrical** (b) **Spherical** (c) **Sferical** (d) **Sferrikle**

9. Scottish writer: Robert Louis …?
(a) **Simpson** (b) **Stevenson** (c) **Burns** (d) **Scott**

Q4

10. Long poem about Heaven and Hell:
(a) **Journey's End** (b) **Paradise Lost** (c) **The Waste Land**
(d) **Canterbury Tales**

Quiz 22 score

Quiz 23

Q1

Your answer | Book answer

1. A black powder:
(a) **Suet** (b) **Suit** (c) **Soot** (d) **Rust**

Q3

2. Which word sounds like water falling?
(a) **Rustle** (b) **Bang** (c) **Rattle** (d) **Splash**

3. Which word means 'comfortable'?
(a) **Posy** (b) **Cosy** (c) **Rosy** (d) **Nosey**

4. Spell the backbone of an animal:
(a) **Spine** (b) **Spyn** (c) **Spinney** (d) **Shin**

Q9

5. A verb meaning to twist threads together:
(a) **Twirl** (b) **Weave** (c) **Burrow** (d) **Unravel**

6. American word for trousers:
(a) **Vest** (b) **Kilt** (c) **Pants** (d) **Tights**

7. A kind of poem:
(a) **Elegy** (b) **Effigy** (c) **Edifice** (d) **Education**

8. Past tense of the verb 'to choose'?
(a) **Choosing** (b) **Choice** (c) **Choosed** (d) **Chose**

9. How many blind mice were there in the rhyme?
(a) **Three** (b) **Four and Twenty** (c) **Two** (d) **Fifty**

10. Which word means 'three times'?
(a) **Once** (b) **Twice** (c) **Thrice** (d) **Quadruple**

Quiz 23 score

Quiz 24

Q1

Your answer | Book answer

1. Which word has to do with aircraft?
(a) **Aeronautics** (b) **Physics** (c) **Oceanography** (d) **Gymnastics**

Q10

2. What's the plural of witch?
(a) **Witchs** (b) **Witchs'** (c) **Witches** (d) **Witch's**

3. Which spelling is correct?
(a) **Dikshunary** (b) **Dikshonerry** (c) **Dictionary** (d)) **Dickshunari**

4. And what does the answer in question 3 mean?
(a) **Book of maps** (b) **Book of words** (c) **Phone book** (d) **Cookery book**

5. Someone who asks for money in the street:
(a) **Beggar** (b) **Prisoner** (c) **Robber** (d) **Shopper**

6. Who picked a peck of pickled peppers?
(a) **Peter Piper** (b) **Little Boy Blue** (c) **Jack Horner** (d) **Silly Sally**

7. Which word describes a cat?
(a) **Canine** (b) **Feline** (c) **Bovine** (d) **Equine**

8. 'The book belonging to Mary': which is correct?
(a) **Marys book** (b) **Mary's book** (c) **Marys' book** (d) **Maryes book**

Q6

9. Which of these ends a question?
(a) **?** (b) **"** (c) **!** (d) **(**

10. Who wrote about Man Friday and Robinson Crusoe?
(a) **Fleming** (b) **Homer** (c) **Defoe** (d) **Cervantes**

Quiz 24 score

Quiz 25

Q1

Your answer | Book answer

1. Means 'as dirty as can be':
(a) **Dirtiest** (b) **Dirty** (c) **Dirtier** (d) **Dirtymost**

Q4

2. Which has the apostrophe in the wrong place?
(a) **Won't** (b) **Shan't** (c) **Cant'** (d) **Haven't**

3. Which words always need a capital letter to start?
(a) **Colours** (b) **Science words** (c) **Town names** (d) **Verbs**

4. Their team is better than ... (fill the gap)
(a) **Its** (b) **Their** (c) **Ours** (d) **My**

5. Which of these is an adjective?
(a) **Slowly** (b) **Clever** (c) **Classroom** (d) **Book**

6. What is the opposite of narrow?
(a) **Wide** (b) **Long** (c) **Thin** (d) **Deep**

Q8

7. The future tense of I am:
(a) **I will be** (b) **I were** (c) **I was** (d) **I have been**

8. Which word rhymes with lunch?
(a) **Branch** (b) **Munch** (c) **Launch** (d) **Grunge**

9. As dull as ... what?
(a) **Monday** (b) **Ditchwater** (c) **Cold pizza** (d) **Doomsday**

10. What's a word list in a book called?
(a) **Summary** (b) **Footnote** (c) **Glossary** (d) **Bibliography**

Quiz 25 score

Quiz 26

Q6

Your answer | Book answer

1. Make an adverb from sad:
(a) **Sadly** (b) **Sadness** (c) **Saddimost** (d) **Saddest**

2. Which word does not mean something to eat?
(a) **Picnic** (b) **Snack** (c) **Sandwich** (d) **Sofa**

Q5

3. Which word rhymes with root?
(a) **Flute** (b) **Rot** (c) **Out** (d) **Lout**

4. Which of these is a noun?
(a) **Terrific** (b) **Tree** (c) **Tremble** (d) **Terrible**

5. A word that rhymes with pulley:
(a) **Frilly** (b) **Hilly** (c) **Pretty** (d) **Woolly**

6. Who was Homer the storyteller?
(a) **A Roman** (b) **A Saxon** (c) **A Spaniard** (d) **A Greek**

7. Sound a mouse might make:
(a) **Screech** (b) **Squawk** (c) **Jingle** (d) **Squeak**

8. Find the adjective:
(a) **Posh** (b) **Pet** (c) **Quickly** (d) **Terror**

Q7

9. Which of these is a noun?
(a) **Wind** (b) **Windy** (c) **Windiest** (d) **To wind**

10. Spell the 'saying it right' word
(a) **Pronunseeation** (b) **Prononsesyashun** (c) **Pronunciation**
(d) **Pronounseeaytion**

Quiz 26 score

Quiz 27

Q4

Your answer | Book answer

1. Which of these can be a noun and a verb?
(a) **Cooker** (b) **Cabbage** (c) **Saucepan** (d) **Bowl**

Q7

2. Spell the thing you swing in:
(a) **Hummock** (b) **Himmok** (c) **Hammock** (d) **Hemlock**

3. Opposite of proper:
(a) **Improper** (b) **Abproper** (c) **Exproper** (d) **Unproper**

4. Can be a tool or fly in the air:
(a) **Plane** (b) **Train** (c) **Drain** (d) **Mane**

5. Who had a friend called Big Ears?
(a) **Eeeyore** (b) **Rupert** (c) **Joseph** (d) **Noddy**

Q2

6. Word meaning a group of ships and a fast runner?
(a) **Fleet** (b) **Fast** (c) **Fling** (d) **Flotilla**

7. A point of balance:
(a) **Pivot** (b) **Divot** (c) **Border** (d) **Summit**

8. 'Trousers of the boys' – which of these is correct?
(a) **Boys trousers** (b) **Boys' trousers** (c) **Boy's trousers** (d) **Boys trousers'**

9. What's the plural of disco?
(a) **Disco** (b) **Disco's** (c) **Discoes** (d) **Discos**

10. A large jug:
(a) **Basin** (b) **Decanter** (c) **Pitcher** (d) **Tumbler**

Quiz 27 score

Super Quiz 28

Q2

1. A form of verse:
(a) **Couple** (b) **Souffle** (c) **Couplet** (d) **Gavotte**

Q3

2. An adjective meaning 'quick and clever':
(a) **Sleek** (b) **Fast** (c) **Brutal** (d) **Brainy**

3. Spell the word correctly (to mean 'writing materials')
(a) **Stashunery** (b) **Stationery** (c) **Stationary** (d) **Stationairy**

4. Which can be a noun and a verb?
(a) **Span** (b) **Spade** (c) **Spa** (d) **Spaghetti**

5. Which is the odd one out (not a writer)?
(a) **David Hockney** (b) **Michael Morpurgo** (c) **Shirley Hughes** (d) **Ted Hughes**

6. Which word means 'red coloured'?
(a) **Aquamarine** (b) **Ruddy** (c) **Azure** (d) **Ashen**

7. Which of these is not a comparative?
(a) **Bigger** (b) **Louder** (c) **Lovely** (d) **Brighter**

8. Spell the stuff you rub on aching muscles:
(a) **Linoleum** (b) **Lingerie** (c) **Linameant** (d) **Liniment**

Q8

9. A prefix meaning 'backward':
(a) **Ergo-** (b) **Intro-** (c) **Extra-** (d) **Retro-**

10. Who or what does a misanthropist hate?
(a) **Everybody** (b) **Animals** (c) **Ants** (d) **Fog**

Your answer | Book answer

Quiz 28 score

Chart Your Scores

	1	2	3	4	5	6	7	8	9	10
Quiz 1										
Quiz 2										
Quiz 3										
Quiz 4										
Quiz 5										
Quiz 6										
Quiz 7										
Quiz 8										
Quiz 9										
Quiz 10										
Quiz 11										
Quiz 12										
Quiz 13										
Quiz 14										
Quiz 15										
Quiz 16										
Quiz 17										
Quiz 18										
Quiz 19										
Quiz 20										
Quiz 21										
Quiz 22										
Quiz 23										
Quiz 24										
Quiz 25										
Quiz 26										
Quiz 27										
Quiz 28										

Answers

Quiz 1
1b, 2b, 3c, 4a, 5c, 6d, 7a, 8b, 9b, 10c

Quiz 2
1b, 2d, 3a, 4b, 5a, 6a, 7d, 8c, 9b, 10d

Quiz 3
1a, 2c, 3b, 4d, 5d, 6d, 7b, 8c, 9b, 10c

Quiz 4
1b, 2c, 3a, 4d, 5b, 6b, 7a, 8a, 9c, 10b

Quiz 5
1c, 2c, 3c, 4a, 5b, 6a, 7c, 8a, 9b, 10a

Quiz 6
1b, 2b, 3b, 4b, 5a, 6a, 7a, 8a, 9b, 10c

Quiz 7
1a, 2d, 3b, 4c, 5a, 6b, 7d, 8c, 9a, 10a

Quiz 8
1c, 2d, 3a, 4b, 5a, 6c, 7b, 8c, 9a, 10c

Quiz 9
1d, 2a, 3b, 4b, 5b, 6c, 7a, 8c, 9d, 10a

Quiz 10
1a, 2c, 3b, 4a, 5c, 6d, 7b, 8d, 9a, 10d

Quiz 11
1b, 2c, 3d, 4a, 5a, 6d, 7c, 8a, 9b, 10a

Quiz 12
1b, 2a, 3d, 4a, 5d, 6b, 7b, 8b, 9c, 10b

Quiz 13
1b, 2c, 3c, 4c, 5b, 6a, 7d, 8b, 9d, 10c

Quiz 14
1d, 2a, 3d, 4a, 5b, 6d, 7d, 8d, 9c, 10b

Quiz 15
1a, 2b, 3d, 4a, 5b, 6c, 7a, 8c, 9c, 10d

Quiz 16
1b, 2c, 3c, 4d, 5a, 6d, 7d, 8a, 9b, 10d

Quiz 17
1a, 2c, 3c, 4a, 5b, 6a, 7c, 8b, 9d, 10b

Quiz 18
1a, 2b, 3c, 4d, 5a, 6b, 7b, 8b, 9b, 10c

Quiz 19
1b, 2d, 3a, 4b, 5a, 6d, 7b, 8b, 9a, 10c

Quiz 20
1c, 2b, 3d, 4d, 5c, 6a, 7b, 8a, 9a, 10d

Quiz 21
1b, 2a, 3c, 4a, 5c, 6d, 7b, 8a, 9b, 10d

Quiz 22
1b, 2a, 3a, 4b, 5c, 6a, 7d, 8b, 9b, 10b

Quiz 23
1c, 2d, 3b, 4a, 5b, 6c, 7a, 8d, 9a, 10c

Quiz 24
1a, 2c, 3c, 4b, 5a, 6a, 7b, 8b, 9a, 10c

Quiz 25
1a, 2c, 3c, 4c, 5b, 6a, 7a, 8b, 9b, 10c

Quiz 26
1a, 2d, 3a, 4b, 5d, 6d, 7d, 8a, 9a, 10c

Quiz 27
1d, 2c, 3a, 4a, 5d, 6a, 7a, 8b, 9d, 10c

Quiz 28
1c, 2b, 3b, 4a, 5a, 6b, 7c, 8d, 9d, 10a